# MOCKTAILS

*Modern Recipes of Fresh Non-Alcoholic Mocktails, Lemonades, and Other Drinks to Make at Home*

**Kathrin Narrell**

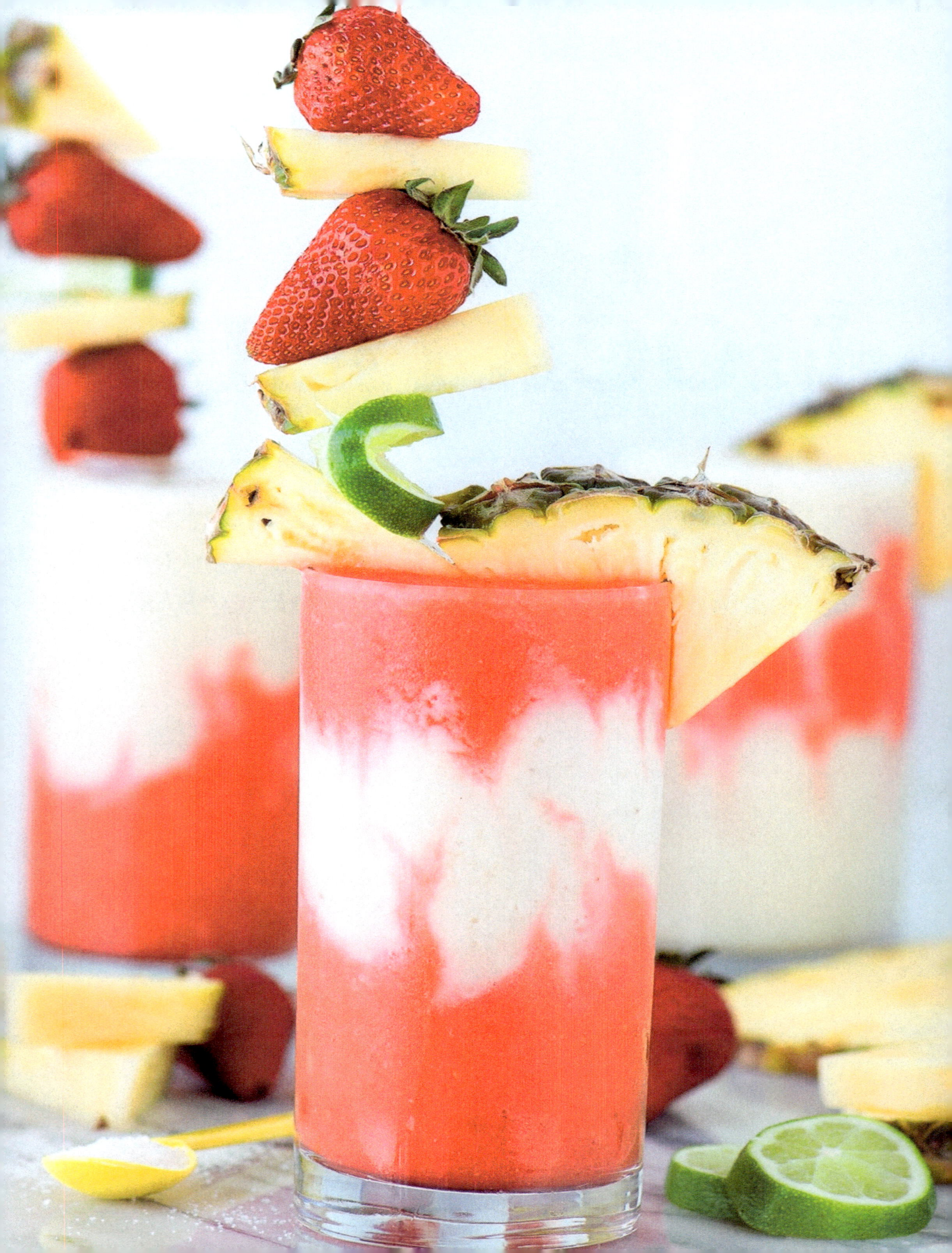

**COPYRIGHT © 2021 BY KATHRIN NARRELL**

**ALL RIGHTS RESERVED.**
No part of this book may be reproduced in any form or by any electronic or mechanical means, except in the case of a brief quotation embodied in articles or reviews, without written permission from its publisher.

**DISCLAIMER**
The recipes and information in this book are provided for educational purposes only. Please always consult a licensed professional before making changes to your lifestyle or diet. The author and publisher shall have neither liability nor responsibility to anyone with respect to any loss or damage caused or alleged to be caused directly or indirectly by the information contained in this book. All trademarks and brands within this book are for clarifying purposes only and are owned by the owners themselves, not affiliated with this document.

Images from shutterstock.com

# CONTENTS

**INTRODUCTION** .................................. 5
**CHAPTER 1. WHY MOVE TO MOCKTAILS?** . 6
**CHAPTER 2. IN THE MOCKTAIL KITCHEN** . 8
   **Tools and Techniques** .................................. 8
   **Essential Ingredients** ................................ 13
**CHAPTER 3. RECIPES** ...................... 15
**MOCKTAILS** ............................................ 15

   Cranberry Sangria .................................. 15
   Negroni Mocktail .................................... 16
   Grapefruit Fizz ....................................... 17
   Shirley Temple Mocktail ........................ 18
   Whipped Lemonade ............................. 19
   Ginger Beer ........................................... 20
   Frozen Virgin Margarita ........................ 21
   Mango Pineapple Slushies ................... 22
   Arnold Palmer Mocktail ........................ 23
   Raspberry Cordial ................................. 24
   Avocado & Berry Mocktail .................... 25
   Cranberry Mocktail ............................... 26
   Melon Fresh Minting Mocktail .............. 27
   Multi Vegetables Mocktail .................... 28
   Rhubarb Mocktail ................................. 29
   Sorrel Mocktail ...................................... 30
   Turmeric Mocktail ................................. 31
   Sorrel & Apple Mocktail ........................ 32
   Cacao Cherry Shake ............................. 33
   Orange Pineapple Shake ...................... 34
   Cold Chocolate ..................................... 35
   Summer Party Punch ............................ 36
   Pumpkin Drink ...................................... 37
   Harsh Tomato ....................................... 38
   Cinnamon Citrus Juice .......................... 39
   Watermelon-Mint Power Drink ............ 40
   Orangeade ............................................ 41
   Ginger Mocktail .................................... 42
   Walnut Milkshake ................................. 43
   Parsley Mocktail ................................... 44

**LEMONADES** .......................................... 45

   Classical Lemonade ............................. 45
   Sparkling Strawberry Lemonade ......... 46
   Pear Lemonade .................................... 47
   Honey Mint Lemonade ........................ 48
   Ginger Iced Lemonade ........................ 49
   Basil & Mint Lemonade ........................ 50
   Cucumber Lemonade .......................... 51
   Lettuce leaves Lemonade .................... 52
   Green Tea Lemonade .......................... 53
   Lavender Lemonade ............................ 54
   Pear Lemonade with Sage ................... 55
   Green Lemonade ................................. 56
   Basil Lemonade ................................... 57
   Rosemary Lemonade .......................... 58
   Mint Lemonade .................................... 59
   Ginger Lemonade ................................ 60
   Raspberry Lemonade .......................... 61
   Strawberry Lemonade ........................ 62
   Blueberry Iced Tea ............................... 63
   Pineapple Orange Punch ..................... 64

**SMOOTHIE DRINKS** ............................... 65

   Strawberry Watermelon Smoothie ...... 65
   Mango Strawberry Smoothie .............. 66
   Pina Colada Spicy Smoothie ................ 67
   Cherry Smoothie .................................. 68
   Mango-Thyme Smoothie ..................... 69
   More-Than-a-Mojito Smoothie ............ 70
   Tropical Pina Colada Smoothie ........... 71
   Green Goddess Smoothie ................... 72
   Mango, Papaya, Raspberry Smoothie .. 73
   Orange Healthy Smoothie ................... 74
   Green Apple Smoothie ........................ 75
   Pumpkin Pie Smoothie ........................ 76
   Raspberry Peach Smoothie ................. 77
   Blueberry Smoothie ............................. 78
   Purple Sage Pineapple Smoothie ........ 79
   Sinless Strawberry Smoothie .............. 80
   Grapefruit Pear Smoothie ................... 81
   Minted Mango Lassi ............................. 82
   Orange, Peach, Kale Smoothie ............ 83
   Oatmeal Fruit Shake ............................ 84

**CONCLUSION** ........................................ 85
**RECIPE INDEX** ...................................... 86
**CONVERSION TABLES** .......................... 87

## INTRODUCTION

Everybody needs a perfect drink that will keep their mind refreshed or will help to relax on a weekend party after a rough week, and mocktails are definitely a perfect choice for these goals! Especially, if you want to avoid a hangover after those fun events!

Why mocktails and no cocktails? The major distinction between mocktails and cocktails is that mocktails are alcohol-free, whereas cocktails are by definition alcoholic. Mocktails, often known as non-alcoholic cocktails, enable you to have a "fun" drink without the negative health effects. Mocktails, like healthy smoothie recipes, are now becoming a method to add extra nutrients and health-boosting effects to your diet.

You may really improve your daily nutritional intake and get all of the advantages of the components you choose to utilize in your homemade mocktail of choice by drinking a well-made and healthy mocktail. Seriously, you may become a whole new person, if you try to quit drinking alcohol with the help of delightful mocktails. Trust me, it's a life-changing substitute!

Doubting mocktail is your dream drink? Yes, these cocktails are alcohol-free, but they're so delicious and refined that you won't miss the party. So, flip this page and let's get started!

# CHAPTER 1. WHY MOVE TO MOCKTAILS?

Mocktails are sometimes a better option than cocktails. The mocktail is a fantastic choice for hot weather, hard exercise, or when you need a non-alcoholic alternative at a party, but it's often neglected. I'll teach you how to prepare non-alcoholic drinks that are easy to make, delicious, and entertaining.

A mocktail is a cocktail that does not include alcohol. Mocktails may be made to look like traditional cocktails like martinis or mojitos, or you can create unique beverages that are flavorful and nutritious. Instead of using liquor, you may make festive and tasty non-alcoholic cocktails by combining juices, sodas, syrups, infused waters, teas, fruits, spices, and countless garnishes. Some mocktails contain ingredients that taste like bourbon, gin, and other alcoholic beverages.

## WHAT ARE THE BENEFITS OF MOCKTAILS?

Mocktails are a fantastic treat to Christmas parties, family dinners, and any other special event. When compared to regular alcoholic beverages, mocktails have several advantages. Here are a few examples:

**Mocktails are often simple and quick to prepare**, and some just require a few ingredients. Without being a professional bartender, you can create amazing mocktails for yourself or visitors.

**Mocktails are far more healthy than cocktails.** Drinking alcohol can have serious consequences for your brain, heart, liver, pancreas, and immune system. Alcohol use also raises the risk of some malignancies, such as liver cancer and breast cancer. Mocktails, on the other hand, can contain substances that are beneficial to your physical and mental health.

Alcoholic beverages are heavy in calories, and they may easily lead to binge eating because they're also intoxicating. You may, however, **prepare mocktails using basic, low-calorie components** while keeping your wits about you to avoid overindulging.

**Because mocktails are alcohol-free, you won't have to worry about losing sleep over your holiday drink.** Alcohol is a depressant, so its sedative effects may make it easier for you to fall asleep. Your liver, on the other hand, will continue to process alcohol throughout the night, disrupting and degrading the quality of your sleep.

**Mocktails are frequently made with healthful components** such as fresh fruit or vegetables, herbs, coconut water, or kombucha. As a result, mocktails let you to engage in the fun while also improving your vitamin C, antioxidant, and other nutrient consumption.

Mocktails can be made using hydrating components such as coconut or mineral water. These drinks can keep you energetic during a party while also preventing dehydration from drinking.

The costliest element in a drink is usually alcohol. You may still enjoy the varied tastes of your beverage while **saving money when you eliminate the alcohol from the recipe**.

After a night or days of drinking, a hangover can make you feel terrible and cause issues at school or at work. Dehydration and inflammation are two elements that lead to a hangover. Mocktails allow you to partake in the festivities without the negative consequences of indulging in alcoholic beverages.

Alcohol reduces inhibitions and affects judgment and decision-making skills, but **mocktails have no effect on decision-making**. Its effects on the brain might put you in danger or disgrace yourself. Each year, more than 10,000 people die as a result of drunk driving, according to the National Highway Traffic Safety Administration. You won't have to worry about your previous night's behavior the next day if you drink mocktails.

**Mocktails are safe for everyone**, including pregnant women, chronically sick people, children, designated drivers, and those in recovery, to enjoy a delightful drink without the dangers of alcohol.

Alcohol is an addictive drug, and more than 14 million persons in the United States suffer from an alcohol use problem. People consume alcohol to get a rush of feel-good endorphins, and they may desire it again despite the harm it causes. **Mocktails eliminate the danger of alcoholism and the difficulties that come with it.**

# CHAPTER 2. IN THE MOCKTAIL KITCHEN

## TOOLS AND TECHNIQUES

### BARTENDING TOOLS

- **BOTTLE OPENER**

A bottle opener is a necessary equipment for every bar. A bottle opener is not required for beer on tap, but it is required for all capped beverages.

- **WATER SPARKLER**

For individuals who want to prepare non-alcoholic beverages on the move but don't have time to drive out to the store for cases of sparkling water, devices like the Soda Stream are lifesavers. They can be more expensive than usual pack of bubbly water, but they will save you money in the long run.

- **COCKTAIL SHAKER**

Liquor, syrups, fruit juices, and ice are generally put in the sealed stainless-steel shaker. Shakers make it simple to pour the drink into the glass after aggressively shaking and mixing it. Many shakers come with built-in strainers to keep ice and other components separate.

- **A STRAINER**

Straining basically means that you strain the mixture through a strainer and it allows you, for example, to eliminate smaller pulp. Just place a fine strainer on top of the serving glass and strain the drink by pouring it.

- **CUTTING BOARDS**

You'll need at least one cutting board to cut cocktail garnishes. Cutting boards not only provide a sanitary and safe cutting surface, but they help keep blades sharp. Choose one that is stable, long-lasting, and non-slip.

### ■ ICE CRUSHER

Many mocktails call for crushed ice. Having an ice crusher is the ideal way to crush ice to the right consistency for your signature mocktails. Alternatively, you can buy crushed ice.

### ■ ICE KIT

Most of the time your ice is going to be cubed, but for some of your signature drinks, you can impress your friends or family with ice cubes in different shapes.

### ■ JIGGER

A jigger should be included in your equipment to ensure that your bartenders are measuring accurately and consistently, not just for taste but also to avoid over-pouring. Choose from jiggers ranging in size from .5oz to 2oz. Or you can easily a measuring cup!

### ■ JUICER

You most likely already have a citrus juicer. It's a basic deep round dish with a cone for squeezing citrus juice. A strainer is sometimes included to separate the pulp from the juice. Fresh juice enhances the flavor of cocktails, so use your citrus juicer at home to obtain fresh juice.

### ■ CITRUS JUICER

You probably already have a citrus juicer. It's a basic deep round dish with a cone for squeezing citrus juice. A strainer is sometimes included to separate the pulp from the juice. Fresh juice enhances the flavor of cocktails, so use your citrus juicer at home to obtain fresh juice.

### ■ MUDDLER

The aromatics of herbs, spices, and fruits are liberated and absorbed into the drink with the help of a quality muddler.

Look for muddlers with long handles and ergonomic designs to make them easier to grip. Dishwasher-safe muddlers are recommended.

### ■ PEELER

A sharp and sturdy peeler is required for those drinks that have a peel garnish. Choose one with an extra-wide carbon steel blade and a non-slip, easy-to-hold grip. It makes peeling citrus fruits safe and simple.

### ■ ZESTER

A sprinkling of lemon or lime on top of various beverages is required, despite the fact that it is not the most commonly utilized equipment behind the bar. All it takes is a fast twist with a zester to add aesthetic appeal and taste to beverages.

### ■ BLENDER

Blenders are primarily used for frozen drinks and are quite useful in making fruit and other purees.

### ■ GLASSES

Cocktail glassware comes in an infinite variety of shapes and sizes. There are a plethora of options. One is more abundant than the other. Clothing is said to make a man, and the same can be said for a drink. Your cocktail will be much more appealing and the focus of everyone's attention if you serve it in a beautiful glass.

### CRAFTING MOCKTAIL TECHNIQUES

#### INFUSIONS

Infusions are a simple and efficient method to add depth to the taste profile of your mocktail. While the term "infusion" may appear complicated, it is actually very frequent and simple. You probably infuse every day when you make coffee or tea!

Infused syrups and infused spirits are the two most frequent infusions. You wouldn't want to make infused spirits because we're preparing mocktails, but you could replace an infused spirit with an infused base, peach tea, and honey. It's all about becoming creative and experimenting with different taste profiles while making a handmade mocktail.

#### OLEO SACCHARUM

You've probably never heard of Oleo Saccharum. Don't be confused by the title. The phrases are latin for "oil sugar," and they refer to the technique of extracting the tasty and fragrant oils from citrus using sugar. Non-alcoholic beverages frequently lack aromatics, and this is a simple method to fix that problem while also adding another layer of wonderful taste.

Making Oleo Saccharum is as simple as it gets: just mix citrus peels with sugar and place in a baggie. Wait a few hours after removing all of the excess air. Voila! Your baggie will be filled with a delectable lemony syrup that begs to be poured into your favorite non-alcoholic beverage.

#### UNUSUAL BASES

Non-alcoholic cocktail recipes are often made with sparkling water, soda, or fruit juice as the foundation. If you want to take your handmade mocktails to the next level, you'll need to think outside the juice – um, box!

While the mentioned bases are relatively prevalent, they are typically tasteless. Experiment with different bases and flavor combinations to make full-bodied non-alcoholic drinks. Chris' Cucumber Water Mint Fauxito recipe is a great example of this. Cucumber juice served as the cocktail's basis, giving it a lovely fragrant and vegetal flavor. Adding mint to the mix elevated it to a whole new level. It's simple and tasty!

## SHRUBS

A non-alcoholic drink prepared with fruit, sugar, aromatics, and vinegar is known as a "shrub." While it may seem strange to incorporate vinegar, it is the vinegar foundation that gives shrubs their acidic and sour flavor without the use of alcohol.

Shrubs provide another option to give "bite" to a drink that would otherwise rely on alcohol. Combining vinegar with sugar and strawberries will revolutionize your mocktail-making techniques.

## "FAUX" BOOZE

If you're attempting to make a non-alcoholic version of your favorite cocktail, there are several "fake" booze choices that might assist. Non-alcoholic spirits can assist retain the taste profile of your favorite drinks while removing the drunken impact.

I'll concede that the flavor characteristics of non-alcoholic spirits and their boozy equivalents aren't precisely the same, but they're close enough.

## AVOID DILUTION

A mocktail's biggest enemy is water. Adding too much water, either directly or via melting ice, is the quickest way to destroy the flavor of your mocktail. To get around this issue, we'll have to think outside the box.

Keep mocktail ice cubes in the freezer instead of adding ice to your drink. Make your favorite mocktail and place it on an ice tray to freeze. Instead of losing taste due to dilution, your ice cubes will add extra flavor!

Another option is to chill your components ahead of time in the fridge, then skip or drastically reduce the shaking / stirring time. Infusion base or mixed fruit cubes can also be frozen!

## USE NON-ALCOHOLIC BITTERS

Bitters have a strong taste and can cut through sweetness like no other. So, if you or your guest wants a cocktail that is completely alcohol-free, you should pick bitters that are alcohol-free with great care.

If you don't mind a smidgeon of alcohol in your drink, you're in luck!

## DON'T FORGET...!

Overall, remember three things: watch your water, watch your sugar and always try to find an inspiration for experiments!

---

There are a lot of simple mocktails to select from, all of which follow the same fundamental concepts or steps:

### "Choose Your Base Liquids"
This is where you must make careful choices, since if you don't, your mocktail will be filled with sugar and empty calories, much like many drinks. Many recipes ask for juice as a basis, but I recommend using a lower-sugar beverage like sparkling mineral water, kombucha, or coconut water instead. Mineral water, of course, is the lowest-sugar choice, with 0 grams of sugar per cup.

If you wish to use a juice as part of or all of your foundation, make sure it's unsweetened and organic. If you utilize freshly squeezed juices, you'll get major extra points.

### "Add Some Whole Fruits"
Now is where you must be very careful because if you want to increase the fiber content and health benefits of your mocktail, select a few pieces of whole fruit that mix well with your base. Organic frozen fruit is a fantastic choice since it helps to cool down your mocktail without diluting it. If you're preparing a savory mocktail, you may include some of your favorite veggies.

### "Fresh Herbs or Spices on Top"
Add herbs or spices to boost the health benefits of your mocktail. These little but powerful components not only boost the health element of your drink, but they also boost the flavor profile. Just like alcoholic drinks, you can add wedges of citrus fruits, citrus peels, or citrus zest.

### "Pick a Perfect Glass"
The goal of the mocktail was to make it feel like you were drinking a cocktail, so pick glassware that matches your mood and recipe. You may use a wine glass, a champagne flute, or a martini glass – whatever makes sense to your merry-go-round.

## ESSENTIAL INGREDIENTS

### INFUSED SYRUPS
Sweeteners with flavor are simple to make: Cook equal parts sugar and water, stirring to dissolve the sugar; infuse with herbs and spices like as ginger, rosemary, or mint, then filter. Refrigerate for up to 2 weeks.

### CITRUSES
Lime or lemon is a staple in most of my mocktails because it combines the sourness of alcohol with the freshness of a drink. You'll see what I mean if you squeeze half a lime over crushed ice and add just about any bubbly alcohol-free drink, excluding beer, of course. Lime should be considered as a vodka substitute. To replace the alcohol base, a shot of lime is added.

### HERBS
Herbs like basil, mint, and cilantro, when muddled, offer a fresh touch to any drink. These herbs go well with infused syrups and compliment most fruit tastes, including lemon, lime, and strawberry. To assist break down the leaves, use a strong muddler and a small amount of sugar or simple syrup in the mixer. Strain your drink into a decorative glass once it's been blended with your chosen juices and/or sodas for a stunning beverage!

### SPARKLING WATER AND OTHERS
Any beverage becomes lighter and more energizing when a natural sparkling component is added. Add a couple of dashes to your drink, and flavored sparkling water if you want an extra boost of flavor. The fizzy, effervescent possibilities are infinite with such a vast range of options accessible.

To make a frothy top layer, add bubbly mixers like tonic water, soda, or ginger beer. Whisked aquafaba, the liquid found in canned chickpeas, has a similar effect and is a popular non-alcoholic beverage.

## Presentation

Serve in appropriate glassware, such as rocks glasses, coupes, and highballs, with decorations such as citrus peels, fresh herbs, and spice rims.

The presentation contributes a lot to the cocktail's appeal. Plant-based garnishes may make your healthy mocktails stand out in addition to the umbrella, fancy straw, huge ice cube, salt rim, or unique glass or mug.

Among them are:
- mint
- edible flowers
- rosemary
- sage
- cucumber
- olives
- citrus wedges
- celery
- berries
- pineapple

### Fruit and Vegetable Purees
Try fruit and veggie bases with less sugar, such as freshly squeezed grapefruit juice, pureed watermelon, or muddled cucumber, instead of bottled juice.

### Shrubs
Shrubs are sour syrups prepared from vinegar, sugar, and fruit or vegetables, sometimes known as drinking vinegar.

### Teas
Herbal teas, such as rooibos and rosehip, are frequently blended with herbs, flowers, spices, and dried fruit, which may add depth to a drink.

### Bitters
A few dashes give beverages depth and sharpness. Although they only contain a little quantity of alcohol, several firms sell nonalcoholic bitters that may be found on the market.

## PLEASE, NOTE!

When you select a mocktail option over a cocktail, you avoid all of the harmful consequences of alcohol. Naturally, avoid making or selecting a mocktail that contains any substances to which you are allergic or sensitive. If a recipe calls for such an item, simply substitute something similar that you know works for you.

Always consult your personal doctor before trying any new juices or mocktail components to your diet if you have any health problems or are using any medications. If you use a blood thinner like warfarin, for example, grapefruit and grapefruit juice are off limits. Diabetics and the rest people with blood sugar issues should be very cautious about the amount of sugar in their mocktails.

# CHAPTER 3. RECIPES
## MOCKTAILS

### CRANBERRY SANGRIA

SERVINGS: 4 | PREP TIME: 10 min. | COOK TIME: none

CARBS: 9 g | FAT: 0 g | PROTEIN: 0 g | CALORIES: 71

### INGREDIENTS

- 1 cup ice cubes
- ¼ pineapple, peeled, sliced
- ½ orange, sliced
- ½ lime, sliced
- 1 passionfruit, quartered
- 2 cups cranberry juice
- 2 cups non-alcoholic ginger beer
- ½ cup fresh mint leaves
- Pomegranate seeds, to serve

### DIRECTIONS

1. Divide your ice among 4 glasses. Place pineapple, orange, lime and passionfruit on top.
2. Divide cranberry juice and ginger beer evenly among prepared glasses.
3. Decorate as desired with cranberries and pomegranate seeds.

# NEGRONI MOCKTAIL

SERVINGS: 1 | PREP TIME: 15 min. | COOK TIME: 5 min.

CARBS: 15 g | FAT: 0 g | PROTEIN: 0 g | CALORIES: 61

## INGREDIENTS

*For the syrup base:*
- ½ grapefruit, chopped into small chunks
- 1 slice orange
- ½ cup caster sugar
- 3 cardamom pods, lightly crushed
- 1 pinch coriander seeds
- 2-3 drops red food colouring (optional)
- ½ cup water

*For the mocktail:*
- Ice, as desired
- 1½ Tbsp white grape juice
- 1 halved slice orange

## DIRECTIONS

1. Put grapefruit chanks, orange slice, sugar, water, cardamom and coriander in a saucepan.
2. Heat everything until it starts simmering, then cook for 5 minutes, crushing softened fruit pieces with the back of a wooden spoon as to release the juices.
3. Once all fruits have softened and white pith has faded, take off from heat and let it cool. Add red food colouring to the syrup if desired.
4. Once syrup is cooled, strain and discard fruits and spices.
5. Add ice in a tumbler and pour in 25ml syrup, grape juice and cold water each. Stir until the outside of tumbler is cold to touch, then decorate with an orange slice.

# GRAPEFRUIT FIZZ

SERVINGS: 8 | PREP TIME: 50 min. | COOK TIME: 5 min.

CARBS: 43 g | FAT: 0 g | PROTEIN: 1 g | CALORIES: 183

## INGREDIENTS

- 1½ cups caster sugar
- 1½ cups ruby red grapefruit juice
- 1½ cups cold water
- 5 cups soda water, chilled
- 1 ruby red grapefruit, peeled, sliced or cut into wedges
- Ice cubes, to serve

## DIRECTIONS

1. Mix sugar and cold water in a saucepan and put it over medium heat. Cook for 5 minutes, stirring, until sugar is dissolved. Then add grapefruit juice and mix well to combine.
2. Transfer prepared mixture to a jug and cover with lid. Put in the fridge and cool completely.
3. Mix with soda water, grapefruit slices and ice once ready to serve.

# SHIRLEY TEMPLE MOCKTAIL

SERVINGS: 4 | PREP TIME: 5 min. | COOK TIME: 5 min.

CARBS: 36 g | FAT: 0 g | PROTEIN: 0 g | CALORIES: 139

## INGREDIENTS

- Ice, as desired
- 3 cups lemon-lime soda
- 1 lime juice
- 4 tsp grenadine
- Maraschino cherries, for serving

## DIRECTIONS

1. Fill 4 serving glasses with ice. Divide lime juice and soda evenly between glasses and place grenadine on top.
2. Decorate each glass with a maraschino cherry and serve.

# WHIPPED LEMONADE

SERVINGS: 4 | PREP TIME: 5 min. | COOK TIME: 5 min.

CARBS: 10 g | FAT: 9 g | PROTEIN: 1 g | CALORIES: 172

## INGREDIENTS

- 1 cup lemonade
- ½ cup sweetened condensed milk
- 1 lemon juice
- 4 cup ice
- lemon slices, for garnish

## DIRECTIONS

1. Mix all components in a blender and blend for 30 seconds -1 minute on high speed until everything is smooth and creamy. Add more ice to adjust thickness if needed.
2. Pour into glasses and top with the lemon slices.

# GINGER BEER

SERVINGS: 6 | PREP TIME: 5 min. | COOK TIME: 5 min.

CARBS: 27 g | FAT: 0 g | PROTEIN: 0 g | CALORIES: 113

## INGREDIENTS

- *1 cup (100g) ginger, scrubbed and roughly chopped*
- *1¼ cups cold water*
- *1 lemon, chopped*
- *½ cup light muscovado sugar*
- *4¼ cup bottle chilled lemonade or sparkling water, to serve*

## DIRECTIONS

1. Add ginger and lemon in a bowl, pour over with cold water and blitz with a blender until very smooth.
2. Strain prepared mixture through a sieve into a bowl, then press the pulp to get as much liquid as possible. Add sugar to the bowl and blitz again.
3. Decant the mixture into a bottle. Chill in the fridge until ready to use. Dilute with chilled lemonade or sparkling water before serving.

# FROZEN VIRGIN MARGARITA

SERVINGS: 6 | PREP TIME: 5 min. | COOK TIME: 5 min.

CARBS: 33 g | FAT: 0 g | PROTEIN: 0 g | CALORIES: 236

## INGREDIENTS

- 2 cups sparkling apple juice
- 1 cup apple & pineapple juice
- 2 tsp finely grated lime rind (optional)
- 2 Tbsp lime juice
- 4 cups ice cubes

## DIRECTIONS

1. Place sparkling apple juice, apple and pineapple juice, lime rind, lime juice and ice in a blender. Blend for 30 seconds up to 1 minute on high speed until smooth. Divide evenly among the glasses.
2. Decorate with lime slices.

# MANGO PINEAPPLE SLUSHIES

SERVINGS: 4 | PREP TIME: 5 min. | COOK TIME: 5 min.

CARBS: 23 g | FAT: 0 g | PROTEIN: 1 g | CALORIES: 91

## INGREDIENTS

- 1 cup frozen mango pieces
- 1 cup frozen pineapple pieces
- 2 cups coconut water
- ⅓ cup lime juice cordial
- 2 cups ice cubes
- ½ cup coconut cream
- Coconut flakes, to serve
- Mint leaves, to serve
- Pineapple, chopped, to serve

## DIRECTIONS

1. Blend pineapple, mango, coconut water and lime cordial in a blender until smooth.
2. Divide ice among 4 serving glasses and top with prepared fruit mixture.
3. Spoon coconut cream on top. Decorate with coconut flakes, chopped pineapple and mint leaves once ready to serve.

# ARNOLD PALMER MOCKTAIL

SERVINGS: 8 | PREP TIME: 10 min. | COOK TIME: 35 min.

CARBS: 22 g | FAT: 0 g | PROTEIN: 0 g | CALORIES: 88

## INGREDIENTS

*For the lemonade:*
- 3 cups water, divided
- ¾ cup granulated sugar
- ¾ cup lemon juice

*For the tea:*
- 4 cups water
- ⅓ cups honey
- 5 black tea bags
- Ice, as desired

## DIRECTIONS

1. To make lemonade, bring 1 cup water and sugar to a boil in a small pot over medium heat, stirring to dissolve sugar. Boil for 2 minutes then cool it to room temperature. Mix prepared syrup, 2 cups water, and lemon juice.
2. To make tea, bring 4 cups water to a boil in a pot over medium-high heat. Add honey and stir well to dissolve. Remove from heat and add tea bags. Let steep 5 minutes. Take tea bags out and cool to room temperature.
3. Mix lemonade and tea in a pitcher. Pour into glasses over ice and serve.

# RASPBERRY CORDIAL

SERVINGS: 6-8 | PREP TIME: 20 min. | COOK TIME: 15 min.

CARBS: 16 g | FAT: 0 g | PROTEIN: 1 g | CALORIES: 78

## INGREDIENTS

- 2 cups raspberry
- 2½ cups caster sugar
- 3 Tbsp red wine vinegar
- 1¼ cup water

## DIRECTIONS

1. Add raspberries, sugar and vinegar in a pan. Mash it over a low heat for 10 minutes until very smooth and looks like a syrup.
2. Rub prepared mixture through a sieve into a clean pan.
3. Remove seeds from the sieve into another bowl and stir together with 1¼ cups water. Sieve again to remove the pulp from seeds.
4. Pour this liquid into the pan with the sieved raspberry pulp, stir well and let it boil for 1 minute.
5. Pour into small sterilized jars or bottles and seal it tightly. Can be stored unopened for a 2-3 months. Once you opened it, store in the fridge.

# AVOCADO & BERRY MOCKTAIL

SERVINGS: 2 | PREP TIME: 1 min. | COOK TIME: none

CARBS: 21 g | FAT: 7.2 g | PROTEIN: 2.7 g | CALORIES: 144

## INGREDIENTS

- *2 cups water*
- *2 cups spinach*
- *1 cup blueberries*
- *1 kiwi*
- *½ avocado*

## DIRECTIONS

1. Combine spinach and water in a blender and pulse on high.
2. Add the remaining ingredients and blend until smooth.

# CRANBERRY MOCKTAIL

SERVINGS: 2 | PREP TIME: 1 min. | COOK TIME: none

CARBS: 16 g | FAT: 0.2 g | PROTEIN: 0.1 g | CALORIES: 72

## INGREDIENTS

- *1 cup cranberries*
- *1 cup apple juice*
- *1 cup water*

## DIRECTIONS

1. Add all ingredients to a blender and pulse on high until smooth.
2. Serve.

# MELON FRESH MINTING MOCKTAIL

SERVINGS: 2 | PREP TIME: 3 min. | COOK TIME: none

CARBS: 31 g | FAT: 1 g | PROTEIN: 3.3 g | CALORIES: 122

## INGREDIENTS

- *2 cups honeydew melon flesh*
- *1½ cups kiwi flesh*
- *10 mint leaves*
- *1 Tbsp lemon juice*
- *2 cups crushed ice*
- *1 tsp stevia*

## DIRECTIONS

1. Add all ingredients to a blender and pulse on high until smooth.
2. Serve.

# MULTI VEGETABLES MOCKTAIL

SERVINGS: 2  |  PREP TIME: 3 min.  |  COOK TIME: none

CARBS: 13 g  |  FAT: 0.2 g  |  PROTEIN: 2.8 g  |  CALORIES: 57

## INGREDIENTS

- *1 bell pepper, deseeded, cored, sliced*
- *1 bunch of spinach, rinsed*
- *2 cups tomato juice*
- *Dash of black pepper*
- *Dash of salt*

## DIRECTIONS

1. Add all ingredients to a blender and pulse on high until smooth.
2. Serve.

# RHUBARB MOCKTAIL

SERVINGS: 1-2 | PREP TIME: 3 min. | COOK TIME: none

CARBS: 26 g | FAT: 0.5 g | PROTEIN: 1.8 g | CALORIES: 108

## INGREDIENTS

- ⅓ whole pineapple, peeled, cored
- 2 rhubarb stalks, peeled, cut in pieces
- 1 cup orange juice
- Fresh mint leaves, to taste (2-4 leaves)

## DIRECTIONS

1. Add all ingredients to a blender and pulse on high until smooth.
2. Serve.

# SORREL MOCKTAIL

SERVINGS: 4 | PREP TIME: 3 min. | COOK TIME: none

CARBS: 27 g | FAT: 0.6 g | PROTEIN: 2 g | CALORIES: 127

## INGREDIENTS

- 1 medium bunch of sorrel, rinsed
- ¼ cup spinach, rinsed
- ½ whole pineapple, peeled, cored, cubed
- 2 oranges, juiced
- ½ lime, juiced

## DIRECTIONS

1. Combine all ingredients in a blender and pulse on high.
2. Serve.

# TURMERIC MOCKTAIL

SERVINGS: 1 | PREP TIME: 1 min. | COOK TIME: none

CARBS: 6 g | FAT: 10 g | PROTEIN: 1 g | CALORIES: 118

## INGREDIENTS

- ½ cup whey
- 1 tsp turmeric powder
- ½ Tbsp flaxseed oil
- ½ cup water
- ½ cup tomato juice
- Dash of black pepper

## DIRECTIONS

1. Combine all ingredients in a blender and pulse on high.
2. Serve.

# SORREL & APPLE MOCKTAIL

SERVINGS: 2 | PREP TIME: 3 min. | COOK TIME: none

CARBS: 41 g | FAT: 0.8 g | PROTEIN: 2.3 g | CALORIES: 166

## INGREDIENTS

- 4 green apples, juiced
- 1 orange, peeled, quartered
- 1 medium bunch sorrel, rinsed

## DIRECTIONS

1. Combine all ingredients in a blender and pulse on high.
2. Serve.

# CACAO CHERRY SHAKE

SERVINGS: 2 | PREP TIME: 3 min. | COOK TIME: none

CARBS: 28 g | FAT: 61 g | PROTEIN: 10 g | CALORIES: 625

## INGREDIENTS

- 2 cups coconut milk
- ½ cup cherries, pitted
- 4 tsp cacao powder
- 2 tsp stevia powder

## DIRECTIONS

1. Add all ingredients to a blender and pulse on high until smooth.
2. Serve.

# ORANGE PINEAPPLE SHAKE

SERVINGS: 2 | PREP TIME: 3 min. | COOK TIME: 5 min.

CARBS: 36 g | FAT: 7 g | PROTEIN: 2 g | CALORIES: 190

## INGREDIENTS

- ½ cup unsweetened almond milk
- ½ cup pineapple juice
- ½ cup low-cholesterol egg product
- 1 cup orange sherbet

## DIRECTIONS

1. Put all the ingredients in a blender. Blend for 30 seconds.
2. Divide into 2 servings.
3. Serve.

# COLD CHOCOLATE

SERVINGS: 3 | PREP TIME: 3 min. | COOK TIME: none

CARBS: 14 g | FAT: 7.7 g | PROTEIN: 5.7 g | CALORIES: 90

## INGREDIENTS

- *1 cup freshly brewed coffee, cooled*
- *4 Tbsp cacao powder*
- *2 Tbsp coconut milk*
- *15 ice cubes*
- *2-3 tsp sweetener*

## DIRECTIONS

1. Add all ingredients to a blender and pulse on high until smooth.
2. Serve.

# SUMMER PARTY PUNCH

SERVINGS: 10 | PREP TIME: 5 min. | COOK TIME: 5 min.

CARBS: 28 g | FAT: 1 g | PROTEIN: 1 g | CALORIES: 196

## INGREDIENTS

*For the punch:*
- *5 cups cranberry juice or cranberry pomegranate juice, chilled*
- *5 cups sparkling apple juice, chilled*

*For the add-ins:*
- *1 orange, halved, sliced then halved again*
- *1 lemon, sliced into rounds*
- *1 cup strawberries, halved or quartered*
- *¾ cup mint leaves*
- *½ cup raspberries*
- *Ice, for serving*

## DIRECTIONS

1. Pour all of the punch components into a large jug or punch bowl.
2. Add the fruit and ice, and stir gently. Don't add too much ice or it will spoil the taste.
3. Serve immediately with a ladle.

# PUMPKIN DRINK

SERVINGS: 1 | PREP TIME: 2 min. | COOK TIME: none

CARBS: 48 g | FAT: 5.5 g | PROTEIN: 3.6 g | CALORIES: 240

## INGREDIENTS

- ½ cup pumpkin purée
- 1 banana, frozen
- 1 cup unsweetened coconut milk
- 1 vanilla bean, split lengthwise, deseeded
- ¼ tsp cinnamon
- ⅛ tsp nutmeg
- ⅛ tsp allspice
- ½ cup ice cubes

## DIRECTIONS

1. In a blender, combine all ingredients.
2. Process until smooth.
3. Serve in a tall glass.

# HARSH TOMATO

SERVINGS: 1 | PREP TIME: 2 min. | COOK TIME: none

CARBS: 11.8 g | FAT: 0.4 g | PROTEIN: 2.3 g | CALORIES: 52

## INGREDIENTS

- 1 cup tomato juice (with salt)
- 1½ tbsp lemon juice
- 2 small celery stalks, cut
- 3 drops Tabasco
- Ice, to taste (usually the ice covers more than half the glass)

## DIRECTIONS

1. Add all ingredients to a blender and pulse on high until smooth.
2. Serve.

# CINNAMON CITRUS JUICE

SERVINGS: 2 | PREP TIME: 5 min. | COOK TIME: 5 min.

CARBS: 27 g | FAT: 0 g | PROTEIN: 2 g | CALORIES: 120

## INGREDIENTS

- 6 oranges, peeled and chopped
- 2 lemons, peeled and chopped
- 1 thumb fresh ginger, peeled
- 2 large carrots, peeled and chopped
- 2 tsp cinnamon
- ¼ cup water
- 1 tsp honey
- 4-6 ice cubes
- 2 cinnamon sticks

## DIRECTIONS

1. Add all ingredients (except ice, cinnamon sticks, and lemon) to the blender.
2. Blend until smooth (20-25 seconds).
3. Strain the juice into a jug.
4. Add ice, lemon, and cinnamon sticks to a glass and pour in the juice.

# WATERMELON-MINT POWER DRINK

SERVINGS: 1 | PREP TIME: 5 min. | COOK TIME: none

CARBS: 23 g | FAT: 5 g | PROTEIN: 13 g | CALORIES: 139

## INGREDIENTS

- *3 cups watermelon, seeded and chopped*
- *5-6 mint leaves*
- *½ cup almond milk*
- *2 Tbsp almond butter*
- *1-2 cups ice cubes*

## DIRECTIONS

1. In a blender, blend all ingredients until smooth.

# ORANGEADE

SERVINGS: **4** | PREP TIME: **15 min.** | COOK TIME: **none**

CARBS: **24 g** | FAT: **0 g** | PROTEIN: **0.6 g** | CALORIES: **94**

## INGREDIENTS

- *1½ cups freshly squeezed orange juice*
- *3 Tbsp agave nectar*
- *4 cups water*

## DIRECTIONS

1. Pour all ingredients into a large pitcher. Stir until the agave nectar dissolves.

# GINGER MOCKTAIL

SERVINGS: 1  |  PREP TIME: 2 min.  |  COOK TIME: none

CARBS: 17 g  |  FAT: 8 g  |  PROTEIN: 8.2 g  |  CALORIES: 171

## INGREDIENTS

- *1 cup kefir, low fat*
- *2 tsp ginger root, grated*
- *1 tsp cinnamon*
- *Dash of red hot pepper*

## DIRECTIONS

1. Add all ingredients to a blender and pulse on high until smooth.
2. Serve.

# WALNUT MILKSHAKE

SERVINGS: 3 | PREP TIME: 8 h. | COOK TIME: none

CARBS: 18 g | FAT: 26 g | PROTEIN: 6.8 g | CALORIES: 323

## INGREDIENTS

- 3 cups cold water, divided
- 1 cup walnuts, soaked overnight
- 1 banana, chopped
- 2 Tbsp oats
- 1 Tbsp vanilla extract
- 1 tsp honey

## DIRECTIONS

1. Put the walnuts into a blender with 1 cup of water and blend. Add remaining water and blend well.
2. Add the remaining ingredients and pulse on high.

# PARSLEY MOCKTAIL

SERVINGS: 1 | PREP TIME: 1 min. | COOK TIME: none

CARBS: 23 g | FAT: 0.6 g | PROTEIN: 2.2 g | CALORIES: 94

## INGREDIENTS

- 1 cup parsley leaves, rinsed
- ½ lemon, peeled, seedless, cut into pieces
- 1 Tbsp honey
- 1¼ cup water

## DIRECTIONS

1. Add all ingredients to a blender and pulse on high until smooth.
2. Serve.

# LEMONADES

## CLASSICAL LEMONADE

SERVINGS: 7 | PREP TIME: 5 min. | COOK TIME: 5 min.

CARBS: 46 g | FAT: 0 g | PROTEIN: 0 g | CALORIES: 179

### INGREDIENTS

- *2 cups granulated sugar*
- *1½ cups fresh lemon juice*
- *4½ - 5 cups water, divided*
- *Ice, for serving*
- *Lemon slices, for serving*

### DIRECTIONS

1. To make the syrup, mix 2 cups of water and sugar in a saucepan over a medium heat. Let it boil and stir to dissolve the sugar. Take off the heat and cool the mixture to room temperature.
2. Strain the lemon juice through a fine-mesh sieve into a 2-quart pitcher. Add the prepared syrup and stir well. Put in the fridge until cold.
3. Before serving, add 2½ cups cold water to the lemonade and stir. Taste, and adjust the sweetness with more water if needed.
4. Serve with ice and sliced lemons.

# SPARKLING STRAWBERRY LEMONADE

SERVINGS: 6 | PREP TIME: 30 min. | COOK TIME: 10 min.

CARBS: 49 g | FAT: 0 g | PROTEIN: 1 g | CALORIES: 202

## INGREDIENTS

- 1 cup lemon juice
- 1 - 1½ cups simple syrup
- 1 16 oz container strawberries, hulled and halved
- 4 cups sparkling water
- Ice cubes
- Mint for garnish

*For the syrup:*

- 2 cups sugar
- 2 cups water

## DIRECTIONS

1. To make the syrup, mix the sugar and water in a saucepan over a medium heat. Bring to a boil. Stir to dissolve the sugar. Let it cool completely.
2. Blend the strawberries with the ½ cup prepared syrup with a hand blender until smooth.
3. Add the lemon juice, ½ cup syrup, strawberry puree, and sparkling water into a lemonade pitcher. Add ice cubes. Chill enough before serving.
4. Add more ice to a glass, pour in the chilled lemonade, garnish with a mint sprig, lemon slice, and strawberry.

# PEAR LEMONADE

SERVINGS: 2  |  PREP TIME: 5 min.  |  COOK TIME: 30 min.

CARBS: 15 g  |  FAT: 1 g  |  PROTEIN: 1 g  |  CALORIES: 50

## INGREDIENTS

- ½ cup ripe pear, peeled and chopped
- 1 cup fresh lemon juice
- ½ cup water

## DIRECTIONS

1. Add pear, lemon juice, and water to a high-speed blender and blend until combined.
2. Refrigerate for 30 minutes.
3. Pour lemonade through a sieve to discard any debris.
4. Serve with ice.

# HONEY MINT LEMONADE

SERVINGS: 7 | PREP TIME: 5 min. | COOK TIME: 5 min

CARBS: 23 g | FAT: 1 g | PROTEIN: 1 g | CALORIES: 86

### INGREDIENTS

- ½ cup honey
- 1 cup lemon juice
- 1 cup fresh mint leaves
- 6 cups cold water
- Lemon slices and additional mint for garnish

### DIRECTIONS

1. Warm 1 cup of water in a small bowl. Add the honey and stir until it has fully dissolved. Add the fresh mint leaves and muddle.
2. Add the rest of the water and lemon juice.
3. Stir until well combined and serve over ice.

# GINGER ICED LEMONADE

SERVINGS: 6 | PREP TIME: 10 min. | COOK TIME: 5 min.

CARBS: 30 g | FAT: 1 g | PROTEIN: 1 g | CALORIES: 113

## INGREDIENTS

- 5 cups filtered water
- 3.5 oz ginger fresh, peeled and chopped
- 1½ cup lemon juice
- ½ cup honey

## DIRECTIONS

1. Add ginger to a pan with water and bring to a boil, then reduce heat and simmer for 5 minutes.
2. Let ginger water cool to lukewarm, then add sweetener and mix well.
3. Mix ginger water and lemon juice in a large jug, and serve.

# BASIL & MINT LEMONADE

SERVINGS: 2 | PREP TIME: 2 h. | COOK TIME: none

CARBS: 2.5 g | FAT: 0.4 g | PROTEIN: 1.3 g | CALORIES: 24

## INGREDIENTS

- *1 bunch basil*
- *1 bunch mint*
- *2 lemons, juiced*
- *4 cups water*
- *1 tsp liquid stevia extract*

## DIRECTIONS

1. Combine water with lemon juice.
2. Add basil and mint leaves to a blender and pulse.
3. Add the blended leaves to lemon water and let stand for 2 hours covered.
4. Filter the lemonade, leaving the leaves behind.
5. Stir in stevia and serve.

# CUCUMBER LEMONADE

SERVINGS: 1 | PREP TIME: 2 min. | COOK TIME: none

CARBS: 15 g | FAT: 0.3 g | PROTEIN: 1.2 g | CALORIES: 90

## INGREDIENTS

- *1 cucumber, cut in chunks*
- *½ lime, juiced*
- *½ orange, juiced*
- *2 sprigs rosemary*
- *1 tsp honey*
- *1 cup water*

## DIRECTIONS

1. Combine all ingredients in a blender and pulse on high.
2. Serve.

# LETTUCE LEAVES LEMONADE

SERVINGS: 2 | PREP TIME: 3 min. | COOK TIME: none

CARBS: 8.8 g | FAT: 0 g | PROTEIN: 2.4 g | CALORIES: 36

## INGREDIENTS

- 4 lettuce leaves, rinsed, torn
- ½ cup mint leaves, rinsed
- 1 lemon, juiced + zest
- 2 cups water
- 10 ice cubes
- ½ tsp stevia extract

## DIRECTIONS

1. Combine all ingredients and pulse on high.
2. Add ice cubes and serve.

# GREEN TEA LEMONADE

SERVINGS: 4 | PREP TIME: 2 min. (+1-2 h. to cool) | COOK TIME: none

CARBS: 3.3 g | FAT: 0.1 g | PROTEIN: 1.1 g | CALORIES: 18

## INGREDIENTS

- 4 cups green tea
- 3 lemons, juiced
- 1 bunch mint leaves, rinsed
- 1 cup water

## DIRECTIONS

1. Combine all ingredients in a jar and put into the fridge until cooled.
2. Serve.

# LAVENDER LEMONADE

SERVINGS: 4 | PREP TIME: 1h. 10 min. (+1-2 h. to cool) | COOK TIME: 5 min.

CARBS: 5.4 g | FAT: 0.6 g | PROTEIN: 0.3 g | CALORIES: 19

## INGREDIENTS

- *2 tbsp dried lavender*
- *3 lemons, juiced*
- *4½ cups water*
- *⅓ stevia extract, liquid*

## DIRECTIONS

1. Add 2½ cups of water into a skillet and bring to boil. Reduce the heat and simmer for 5 minutes. Remove from heat and let stand for 1 hour covered.
2. Filter out the lavender flowers, and add lemon juice, water, and stevia.
3. Pour the lemonade into a jar and place into the fridge to cool.

# PEAR LEMONADE WITH SAGE

SERVINGS: 1 | PREP TIME: 3 min. | COOK TIME: none

CARBS: 12.2 g | FAT: 0.3 g | PROTEIN: 0.8 g | CALORIES: 52

## INGREDIENTS

- *1 Tbsp fresh sage leaves*
- *½ lime, sliced*
- *¼ cup sparkling water*
- *½ cup pear juice*
- *Crushed ice*

## DIRECTIONS

1. Put lime slice and sage leaves into a tumbler.
2. Add a couple of tablespoons of crushed ice.
3. Pour in the pear juice and sparkling water.
4. Decorate with sage leaf or lime slice.

# GREEN LEMONADE

SERVINGS: 2 | PREP TIME: 7 min. | COOK TIME: none

CARBS: 13 g | FAT: 1 g | PROTEIN: 3.4 g | CALORIES: 66

## INGREDIENTS

- *4 cucumbers*
- *4 celery stalks*
- *1 lemon*
- *1 cup collard greens*
- *1 cup water*

## DIRECTIONS

1. Juice all ingredients and combine the juices with water.
2. Serve cool.

# BASIL LEMONADE

SERVINGS: 3 | PREP TIME: 3 min. (+1h. to cool) | COOK TIME: none

CARBS: 16.5 g | FAT: 0.3 g | PROTEIN: 1.2 g | CALORIES: 47

## INGREDIENTS

- *1 bunch basil leaves*
- *7 limes, quartered*
- *3 cups water*
- *1¼ tsp stevia powdered extract*
- *9 ice cubes*

## DIRECTIONS

1. Place the basil leaves and stevia into a jar and crush together.
2. Juice the limes into the jar. Add the rind to the jar too.
3. Add water.
4. Add crushed ice and cool in the fridge.
5. Serve.

# ROSEMARY LEMONADE

SERVINGS: 2 | PREP TIME: 15 min. (+1-2 h. to cool) | COOK TIME: 5 min.

CARBS: 8.8 g | FAT: 0.4 g | PROTEIN: 1.1 g | CALORIES: 29

## INGREDIENTS

- *2 sprigs rosemary*
- *½ tsp ginger*
- *3 lemons, juice + zest*
- *2 cups water*
- *12 drops liquid stevia*
- *Ice, to taste (usually more than half glass covered)*

## DIRECTIONS

1. In a pan, combine water, lemon peel, and 1 rosemary sprig. Bring to boil. Then boil for 5 min.
2. Remove from heat and filter out the peel and the sprig.
3. Add ginger and let cool.
4. Stir in stevia and lemon juice.
5. Put a rosemary sprig and some lemon slices into a jar and pour the lemonade into it.
6. Cool in the fridge.

# MINT LEMONADE

SERVINGS: 3 | PREP TIME: 1h. 3 min. | COOK TIME: 3 min.

CARBS: 5.7 g | FAT: 0.2 g | PROTEIN: 0.8 g | CALORIES: 19

## INGREDIENTS

- 2 lemons, juiced
- ½ cup fresh mint leaves, chopped
- 1 tsp stevia, liquid
- 4 cups sparkling water

## DIRECTIONS

1. Combine all ingredients and let stand in the fridge for 1 hour.
2. Filter and serve.

# GINGER LEMONADE

SERVINGS: 1 cup | PREP TIME: 15 min. | COOK TIME: 2 min.

CARBS: 16 g | FAT: 2.1 g | PROTEIN: 2.3 g | CALORIES: 97

## INGREDIENTS

- ½ cup water
- ½ cup lemon juice
- 2-inch piece ginger, peeled, sliced
- 1 tsp liquid stevia
- Sparkling water
- Ice (usually more than half glass covered)

## DIRECTIONS

1. In a pot, combine water, sweetener, and ginger. Bring to a boil, and remove from heat and let cool.
2. Add lemon juice.
3. Strain the mixture into a jar and store in the fridge.
4. To serve, take some lemon ginger syrup and mix with sparkling water and ice.

# RASPBERRY LEMONADE

SERVINGS: 3 | PREP TIME: 2 min. | COOK TIME: none

CARBS: 6.6 g | FAT: 0.9 g | PROTEIN: 1.1 g | CALORIES: 41

## INGREDIENTS

- 1 cup raspberry
- 1 cup lemon juice
- 3 cups water
- Ice, to taste (usually more than half glass covered)

## DIRECTIONS

1. Blend 1 cup raspberry with 3/4 cup water.
2. Strain mixture, keeping only the liquid.
3. Combine raspberry water, lemon juice, water, and ice.

# STRAWBERRY LEMONADE

**SERVINGS:** 12 | **PREP TIME:** 5 min. | **COOK TIME:** 10 min.

**CARBS:** 23 g | **FAT:** 0 g | **PROTEIN:** 0 g | **CALORIES:** 87

## INGREDIENTS

- *8 large strawberries, halved*
- *2 Tbsp white sugar*
- *7 cups water, divided*
- *1 cup white sugar*
- *2 cup lemon juice*
- *Fresh mint leaves, for serving*

## DIRECTIONS

1. Add the strawberries to a blender and top with 2 Tbsp sugar. Pour 1 cup of water over the berries. Blend for 1 minute until it's juicy with no chunks.
2. Mix the strawberry juice, 1 cup of sugar, 6 cups of water, and lemon juice in a pitcher. Stir well.
3. Let it chill before serving.
4. Top with fresh mint leaves and enjoy.

# BLUEBERRY ICED TEA

SERVINGS: 6 | PREP TIME: 1 day | COOK TIME: 5 min.

CARBS: 10 g | FAT: 0 g | PROTEIN: 0 g | CALORIES: 40

## INGREDIENTS

- 2 cups fresh blueberries, more for serving
- 4 black tea bags
- 2 cups sugar
- 1 lemon juice and wedges
- 7½ cups water
- 3–4 fresh mint leaves

## DIRECTIONS

1. Add ½ a cup of water and the blueberries to a saucepan over a medium–high heat.
2. Once it is boiling, cook for 3 minutes.
3. Mash the cooked blueberries. Strain the mashed fruit juice into a bowl.
4. Squeeze the blueberry juice into the bowl using the back of a spoon.
5. Pour the blueberry juice, lemon juice, water, and mint leaves into the pitcher.
6. Mix well and add the tea bags. Put in the fridge overnight.
7. Add ice to each glass, then the fresh blueberries, and pour in the blueberry juice.
8. Top with fresh mint leaves and lemon wedges before serving.

MOCKTAILS | 63

# PINEAPPLE ORANGE PUNCH

SERVINGS: 8 | PREP TIME: 5 min. | COOK TIME: 5 min.

CARBS: 22 g | FAT: 0 g | PROTEIN: 1 g | CALORIES: 90

## INGREDIENTS

- 2 cups unsweetened pineapple juice
- 2 cups orange juice (juice, not concentrate)
- 2 Tbsp key lime juice
- 2 cups Sprite
- Fresh raspberries and blueberries
- Orange slices

## DIRECTIONS

1. Mix the pineapple, orange, and lime juice in a pitcher or punch bowl. Refrigerate for 4-5 hours to chill it enough.
2. When ready to serve, stir in Sprite. Then, add berries and orange slices to the pitcher or punch bowl.
3. Serve immediately.

# SMOOTHIE DRINKS

## STRAWBERRY WATERMELON SMOOTHIE

SERVINGS: 4 | PREP TIME: 5 min. | COOK TIME: 5 min.

CARBS: 22 g | FAT: 0 g | PROTEIN: 1 g | CALORIES: 87

### INGREDIENTS

- *2 cups strawberries, stems removed*
- *2 cups ice*
- *1 cup watermelon*
- *1 cup vanilla Greek yogurt*
- *½ cup coconut milk*
- *1 tsp ground flax seed*
- *4 strawberries, for serving*

### DIRECTIONS

1. Add the strawberries, watermelon, yogurt, ice, and flax seeds to a blender.
2. Blend the mixture for 30 seconds or so until smooth.
3. Pour into glasses and decorate with strawberries.
4. Serve immediately!

# MANGO STRAWBERRY SMOOTHIE

SERVINGS: 1 | PREP TIME: 5 min. | COOK TIME: 5 min.

CARBS: 75 g | FAT: 2 g | PROTEIN: 6 g | CALORIES: 296

## INGREDIENTS

- *1 medium banana, frozen*
- *½ cup mango, frozen*
- *½ cup strawberries, frozen*
- *½ cup pineapple, fresh or frozen*
- *1 cup coconut water or filtered water*
- *1 juice of a lemon (optional)*

## DIRECTIONS

1. Prepare all fruits for the smoothie overnight.
2. Add all ingredients to a blender.
3. Blend on a high speed for 1 minute.
4. Serve with strawberry slice.
5. Enjoy!

# PINA COLADA SPICY SMOOTHIE

SERVINGS: 2  |  PREP TIME: 2 min.  |  COOK TIME: 5 min.

CARBS: 13 g  |  FAT: 32 g  |  PROTEIN: 5 g  |  CALORIES: 189

## INGREDIENTS

- *1 cup Mascarpone Cheese firm*
- *1 cup pineapple, canned or fresh*
- *1 tsp Stevia or another sweetener*
- *½ cup pineapple juice, unsweetened*
- *Pinch red pepper flakes*

## DIRECTIONS

1. Mix all the ingredients in a blender.
2. Serve.

# CHERRY SMOOTHIE

SERVINGS: 1 | PREP TIME: 10 min. | COOK TIME: none

CARBS: 52 g | FAT: 2 g | PROTEIN: 3 g | CALORIES: 256

## INGREDIENTS

- *1 cup frozen unsweetened pitted cherries*
- *¼ cup raspberries*
- *¾ cup coconut water*
- *1 tbsp raw honey or maple syrup*
- *1 tsp chia seeds*
- *1 tsp hemp seeds*
- *Drop vanilla extract*

## DIRECTIONS

1. In a blender, combine the cherries, raspberries, coconut water, honey, chia seeds and hemp seeds.
2. Add vanilla and blend until smooth.

# MANGO-THYME SMOOTHIE

SERVINGS: 1 | PREP TIME: 10 min. | COOK TIME: none

CARBS: 65 g | FAT: 4 g | PROTEIN: 3 g | CALORIES: 274

## INGREDIENTS

- 1 cup mango chunks
- ½ cup white, seedless grapes
- ¼ fennel bulb
- ½ cup unsweetened almond milk
- ½ tsp fresh thyme leaves
- Salt, pepper to taste

## DIRECTIONS

1. In a blender, combine the mango, grapes, fennel, almond milk, thyme leaves, sea salt, and pepper. Blend until smooth.

# MORE-THAN-A-MOJITO SMOOTHIE

SERVINGS: 1 | PREP TIME: 2 min. | COOK TIME: none

CARBS: 61 g | FAT: 1.5 g | PROTEIN: 2.6 g | CALORIES: 241

## INGREDIENTS

- *1 cup spinach*
- *1 cup unsweetened coconut water*
- *2 cups pineapple*
- *2 Tbsp fresh mint leaves*
- *Juice of ½ lime*

## DIRECTIONS

1. In a blender, combine all ingredients.
2. Process until smooth.
3. Serve in a tall glass.

# TROPICAL PINA COLADA SMOOTHIE

SERVINGS: 1 | PREP TIME: 2 min. | COOK TIME: none

CARBS: 39 g | FAT: 3.2 g | PROTEIN: 2 g | CALORIES: 175

## INGREDIENTS

- ½ cup unsweetened coconut milk
- 2½ cups fresh pineapple chunks
- 1 cup ice cubes

## DIRECTIONS

1. Add all ingredients to a blender.
2. Blend until smooth.
3. Divide into two portions and serve.

# GREEN GODDESS SMOOTHIE

SERVINGS: 2 | PREP TIME: 10 min. | COOK TIME: none

CARBS: 16 g | FAT: 20 g | PROTEIN: 4 g | CALORIES: 245

## INGREDIENTS

- *1 large avocado, peeled, pitted and chopped*
- *2 cups romaine lettuce, chopped*
- *1 cup fresh baby spinach*
- *1 cup fresh baby kale*
- *¼ cup fresh mint leaves*
- *4 Tbsp fresh lemon juice*
- *6 drops liquid stevia*
- *2 cups filtered water*
- *½ cup ice cubes*

## DIRECTIONS

1. In a blender, pulse all ingredients until smooth.
2. Transfer into 2 serving glasses and serve immediately.

# MANGO, PAPAYA, RASPBERRY SMOOTHIE

SERVINGS: 1 | PREP TIME: 2 min. | COOK TIME: none

CARBS: 40 g | FAT: 0 g | PROTEIN: 2 g | CALORIES: 153

## INGREDIENTS

- ¼ cup raspberries
- ¾ cup frozen mango pieces
- ½ medium papaya, seeds removed, chopped

## DIRECTIONS

1. In a blender, combine all ingredients.
2. Process until smooth.
3. Serve in a tall glass.

# ORANGE HEALTHY SMOOTHIE

SERVINGS: 1 | PREP TIME: 2 min. | COOK TIME: none

CARBS: 44 g | FAT: 0 g | PROTEIN: 2.3 g | CALORIES: 182

## INGREDIENTS

- 6 ounces freshly squeezed orange juice
- 1 ounce unsweetened coconut milk
- 1 medium frozen banana, cut into chunks
- 1 vanilla bean, split lengthwise, deseeded
- 1 packet stevia

## DIRECTIONS

1. In a blender, combine all ingredients.
2. Process until smooth.
3. Serve in a tall glass.

# GREEN APPLE SMOOTHIE

SERVINGS: 1  |  PREP TIME: 10 min.  |  COOK TIME: none

CARBS: 41 g  |  FAT: 1 g  |  PROTEIN: 2 g  |  CALORIES: 176

## INGREDIENTS

- ½ cup coconut water
- 1 green apple, peeled, cored, seeded, quartered
- 1 cup spinach
- ¼ lemon, seeded
- ½ cucumber, peeled, seeded
- 2 tsp raw honey

## DIRECTIONS

1. In a blender, combine the coconut water, apple, spinach, lemon, cucumber, and honey. Blend until smooth.

# PUMPKIN PIE SMOOTHIE

SERVINGS: 2  |  PREP TIME: 5 min.  |  COOK TIME: none

CARBS: 30 g  |  FAT: 2.5 g  |  PROTEIN: 5 g  |  CALORIES: 150

## INGREDIENTS

- *1 cup pumpkin puree*
- *1 large ripe banana*
- *1 cup unsweetened soy milk*
- *2 pitted dates*
- *½ tsp pure vanilla extract*
- *1 ¼ tsp pumpkin pie spice*
- *5 ice cubes*
- *½ tsp ground flaxseeds*
- *Pinch of nutmeg*

## DIRECTIONS

1. Mix all ingredients in a blender and blend until smooth.

# RASPBERRY PEACH SMOOTHIE

SERVINGS: 3 | PREP TIME: 5 min. | COOK TIME: 5 min.

CARBS: 23 g | FAT: 6.3 g | PROTEIN: 3.2 g | CALORIES: 129

## INGREDIENTS

- *1 medium peach, sliced*
- *1 cup frozen raspberries*
- *1 tablespoon honey*
- *½ cup tofu*
- *1 cup unfortified almond milk*

## DIRECTIONS

1. Mix all the ingredients in your blender.
2. Enjoy!

# BLUEBERRY SMOOTHIE

SERVINGS: 3 | PREP TIME: 5 min. | COOK TIME: 2 min.

CARBS: 31 g | FAT: 7.5 g | PROTEIN: 0.7 g | CALORIES: 155

## INGREDIENTS

- 2 cups frozen blueberries (slightly thawed)
- 1¼ cup pineapple juice
- 2 tsp sugar or Splenda
- ¾ cup pasteurized egg whites
- ½ cup water

## DIRECTIONS

1. Mix all the ingredients in blender and puree.

# PURPLE SAGE PINEAPPLE SMOOTHIE

SERVINGS: 2 | PREP TIME: 5 min. | COOK TIME: 5 min.

CARBS: 23 g | FAT: 6 g | PROTEIN: 5 g | CALORIES: 143

## INGREDIENTS

- 1 oz blackberries
- 2 oz pineapple
- 1 apple, chopped
- 2 sprigs sage
- ½ tsp maqui berry powder
- 2 tbsp walnuts
- 1 cup water
- 1 cup ice

## DIRECTIONS

1. Add berries and rest ingredients to a blender.
2. Blend for 1 minute on high.
3. Enjoy!

# SINLESS STRAWBERRY SMOOTHIE

SERVINGS: 1 | PREP TIME: 10 min. | COOK TIME: none

CARBS: 46 g | FAT: 1 g | PROTEIN: 15 g | CALORIES: 251

## INGREDIENTS

- ½ cup fat-free vanilla ice cream
- 1 cup fresh strawberries
- ½ cup nonfat yogurt
- ½ cup skim milk

## DIRECTIONS

1. Combine all ingredients in a blender until smooth. Pour into a tall glass.

# GRAPEFRUIT PEAR SMOOTHIE

SERVINGS: 2 | PREP TIME: 10 min. | COOK TIME: 10 min.

CARBS: 27 g | FAT: 0 g | PROTEIN: 2 g | CALORIES: 108

## INGREDIENTS

- 1 pear, chopped
- 1 orange, chopped
- 1 grapefruit, chopped
- 1 piece ginger, chopped
- 1 large handful spinach
- ½ cup water

## DIRECTIONS

1. Blend the spinach with the water.
2. Then add the remaining ingredients to the blender.
3. Blend until smooth.
4. Divide evenly between 2 glasses.
5. Enjoy!

# MINTED MANGO LASSI

SERVINGS: 2 | PREP TIME: 3 min. | COOK TIME: none

CARBS: 34 g | FAT: 3 g | PROTEIN: 7 g | CALORIES: 79

## INGREDIENTS

- *1 mango*
- *1 cup plain or soy yogurt*
- *3 cups water*
- *1 handful fresh mint*

## DIRECTIONS

1. In a blender, combine all ingredients until smooth.
2. Pour into 2 glasses and serve.

# ORANGE, PEACH, KALE SMOOTHIE

SERVINGS: 1 | PREP TIME: 10 min. | COOK TIME: none

CARBS: 38 g | FAT: 0 g | PROTEIN: 4.6 g | CALORIES: 158

## INGREDIENTS

- *1 orange, peeled, seeded*
- *1 medium peach, peeled, sliced*
- *1 cup kale, chopped*
- *8 ounces filtered water*

## DIRECTIONS

1. In a blender, combine all ingredients.
2. Process until smooth.
3. Serve in a tall glass.

# OATMEAL FRUIT SHAKE

SERVINGS: 2 | PREP TIME: 10 min. | COOK TIME: none

CARBS: 58 g | FAT: 1.5 g | PROTEIN: 5 g | CALORIES: 270

## INGREDIENTS

- 1 cup oatmeal, already prepared and cooled
- 1 apple, cored and roughly chopped
- 1 banana, halved
- 1 cup baby spinach
- 2 cups coconut water
- 2 cups ice, cubed
- ½ tsp ground cinnamon
- 1 tsp pure vanilla extract

## DIRECTIONS

1. Add all ingredients to blender.
2. Blend from low to high for several minutes until smooth.

# CONCLUSION

Thank you for reading this book and having the patience to try the recipes.

I do hope that you have had as much enjoyment reading and experimenting with the meals as I have had writing the book.

If you would like to leave a review, you can do so at Your Orders section in your Amazon account or using QR-code providing below.

**Stay safe and healthy!**

# RECIPE INDEX

## A

Arnold Palmer Mocktail ................................. 23
Avocado & Berry Mocktail ............................. 25

## B

Basil & Mint Lemonade .................................. 50
Basil Lemonade ............................................. 57
Blubbery Iced Tea .......................................... 63
Blueberry Smoothie ....................................... 78

## C

Cacao Cherry Shake ....................................... 33
Cherry Smoothie ............................................ 68
Cinnamon Citrus Juice ................................... 39
Classical Lemonade ....................................... 45
Cold Chocolate .............................................. 35
Cranberry Mocktail ........................................ 26
Cranberry Sangria .......................................... 15
Cucumber Lemonade .................................... 51

## F

Frozen Virgin Margarita ................................. 21

## G

Ginger Beer .................................................... 20
Ginger Iced Lemonade ................................... 49
Ginger Lemonade .......................................... 60
Ginger Mocktail ............................................. 42
Grapefruit Fizz ............................................... 17
Grapefruit Pear Smoothie .............................. 81
Green Apple Smoothie .................................. 75
Green Goddess Smoothie .............................. 72
Green Lemonade ........................................... 56
Green Tea Lemonade ..................................... 53

## H

Harsh Tomato ................................................ 38
Honey Mint Lemonade .................................. 48

## L

Lavender Lemonade ...................................... 54
Lettuce leaves Lemonade .............................. 52

## M

Mango Pineapple Slushies ............................. 22
Mango Strawberry Smoothie ......................... 66
Mango, Papaya, Raspberry Smoothie ............ 73
Mango-Thyme Smoothie ............................... 69
Melon Fresh Minting Mocktail ....................... 27

Mint Lemonade ............................................. 59
Minted Mango Lassi ...................................... 82
More-Than-a-Mojito Smoothie ...................... 70
Multi Vegetables Mocktail ............................. 28

## N

Negroni Mocktail ........................................... 16

## O

Oatmeal Fruit Shake ...................................... 84
Orange Healthy Smoothie ............................. 74
Orange Pineapple Shake ............................... 34
Orange, Peach, Kale Smoothie ...................... 83
Orangeade ..................................................... 41

## P

Parsley Mocktail ............................................ 44
Pear Lemonade ............................................. 47
Pear Lemonade with Sage ............................. 55
Pina Colada Spicy Smoothie .......................... 67
Pineapple Orange Punch ............................... 64
Pumpkin Drink ............................................... 37
Pumpkin Pie Smoothie .................................. 76
Purple Sage Pineapple Smoothie .................. 79

## R

Raspberry Cordial .......................................... 24
Raspberry Lemonade .................................... 61
Raspberry Peach Smoothie ........................... 77
Rhubarb Mocktail .......................................... 29
Rosemary Lemonade .................................... 58

## S

Shirley Temple Mocktail ................................ 18
Sinless Strawberry Smoothie ........................ 80
Sorrel & Apple Mocktail ................................ 32
Sorrel Mocktail .............................................. 30
Sparkling Strawberry Lemonade ................... 46
Strawberry Lemonade ................................... 62
Strawberry Watermelon Smoothie ................ 65
Summer Party Punch .................................... 36

## T

Tropical Pina Colada Smoothie ..................... 71
Turmeric Mocktail ......................................... 31

## W

Walnut Milkshake .......................................... 43
Watermelon-Mint Power Drink ..................... 40
Whipped Lemonade ...................................... 19

# CONVERSION TABLES

## Dry Weights

| OZ | Tbsp | C | g | lb |
|---|---|---|---|---|
| 1/2 OZ | 1 Tbsp | 1/16 C | 15 g | |
| 1 OZ | 2 Tbsp | 1/8 C | 28 g | |
| 2 OZ | 4 Tbsp | 1/4 C | 57 g | |
| 3 OZ | 6 Tbsp | 1/3 C | 85 g | |
| 4 OZ | 8 Tbsp | 1/2 C | 115 g | 1/4 lb |
| 8 OZ | 16 Tbsp | 1 C | 227 g | 1/2 lb |
| 12 OZ | 24 Tbsp | 1 1/2 C | 340 g | 3/4 lb |
| 16 OZ | 32 Tbsp | 2 C | 455 g | 1 lb |

## Liquid Conversions

**1 Gallon:** 4 quarts, 8 pints, 16 cups, 128 fl oz, 3.8 liters

**1 Quart:** 2 pints, 4 cups, 32 fl oz, 0.95 liters

**1 Pint:** 2 cups, 16 fl oz, 480 ml

**1 Cup:** 16 Tbsp, 8 fl oz, 240 ml

| oz | tsp | Tbsp | mL | C | Pt | Qt |
|---|---|---|---|---|---|---|
| 1 oz | 6 tsp | 2 Tbsp | 30 ml | 1/8 C | | |
| 2 oz | 12 tsp | 4 Tbsp | 60 ml | 1/4 C | | |
| 2 2/3 oz | 16 tsp | 5 Tbsp | 80 ml | 1/3 C | | |
| 4 oz | 24 tsp | 8 Tbsp | 120 ml | 1/2 C | | |
| 5 1/3 oz | 32 tsp | 11 Tbsp | 160 ml | 2/3 C | | |
| 6 oz | 36 tsp | 12 Tbsp | 177 ml | 3/4 C | | |
| 8 oz | 48 tsp | 16 Tbsp | 237 ml | 1 C | 1/2 pt | 1/4 qt |
| 16 oz | 96 tsp | 32 Tbsp | 480 ml | 2 C | 1 pt | 1/2 qt |
| 32 oz | 192 tsp | 64 Tbsp | 950 ml | 4 C | 2 pt | 1 qt |

## Fahrenheit to Celcius (F to C)

500 F = 260 C
475 F = 245 C
450 F = 235 C
425 F = 220 C
400 F = 205 C
375 F = 190 C
350 F = 180 C
325 F = 160 C
300 F = 150 C
275 F = 135 C
250 F = 120 C
225 F = 107 C

1 tsp: 5 ml
1 Tbsp: 15 ml

## Safe Cooking Meat Temperatures

**Minimum temperatures:**

**USDA Safe at 145 F** — Beef Steaks, Briskets, and Roasts; Pork Chops, Roasts, Ribs, Shoulders, and Butts; Lamb Chops, Legs, and Roasts; Fresh Hams, Veal Steaks, Fish, and Shrimp

**USDA Safe at 160 F** — Ground Meats (except poultry)

**USDA Safe at 165 F** — Chicken & Turkey, ground or whole

Printed in Great Britain
by Amazon